HOLY SPIRIT EMPOWERED

Holy Spirit Empowered

CYNTHIA GREELY

PURELILLY PRESS

Contents

ISBN: 979-8-9879012-2-9

Published by Purelilly Press Publishing
Huntsville, Texas

Unless otherwise noted, scripture quotations are from the Holy Bible, New International Version, copyright © 1973, 1978, 1984 by International Bible Society.
Quotations identified NKJV are from the Holy Bible, New King James Version, copyright © 1979, 1980, 1982, by Thomas Nelson, Inc., Publishers.
Quotations identified KJV are from the Holy Bible, King James Version.
All uses of italics in biblical text have been added by the author for emphasis.

First Printing, 2024

Preface

Welcome To Holy Spirit Empowerment!

Speaking From My Heart

Dear Friends,

Welcome to this journey of discovering the empowering power of the Holy Spirit. This book holds a special place close to my heart as I share testimonies that have helped Me Through my journey. As I began writing this book, I experienced a profound season of spiritual warfare and personal challenges. Every time I sat down to write, it was a fantastic instance. From sudden disruption to overwhelming feelings of doubt and inadequacy, the enemy sought to hinder God's message in my heart. There were moments when I questioned if I could continue, but the Holy Spirit provided the strength and inspiration I needed to persevere each time I sat down to write.

Ultimately, I understood that this season of challenges was not permanent. It was a time of refinement and growth, during which I learned to rely more deeply on God's power and presence. I emerged from this season with a renewed sense of purpose and more assertive faith than I had ever experienced before. I know that through the empowerment of the Holy Spirit, I am ready to share the incredible testimonies of God's work in my life.

Prologue

Believe in Yourself

Believing in yourself isn't just about relying on your strength and abilities. It's about knowing deep down that you are uniquely crafted by God, created with a purpose that only you can fulfill. When you realize that God has given you everything you need to live out that purpose, it changes how you see yourself. By trusting in the Holy Spirit, you're connecting with a source of strength, wisdom, and guidance far beyond what you could ever achieve on your own. It's about recognizing that God has created you with a unique purpose and has equipped you with everything you need to fulfill that purpose. When you trust in the power of the Holy Spirit, you tap into a source of strength, wisdom, and guidance that transcends human limitations.

Encouragement for You

As you read this book, I encourage you to open your heart to the possibilities God has for you. Believe in the unique gifts and abilities He has given you. Trust that the Holy Spirit is ready to empower you in every aspect of your life. Remember, you are not alone. God is with you, and His Spirit is at work within you, providing the strength and guidance you need.

It's essential to believe that God can work powerfully through you and trust that He is faithful to do what He says. God always keeps His word. That's why it's so important to plant His Word deep in your heart. You can do this by meditating on and learning key scriptures, letting them guide you in your daily life.

Key Scriptures to Empower and Motivate You

I can do all this through him who gives me the strength.

- Philippians 4:13 (NKJV)

Let this verse remind you that your ability to overcome challenges comes from Christ's strength working in you.

He gives strength to the weary and increases the power of the weak..but those who hope in the Lord will renew their strength.

- Isaiah 40:29, 31

When you feel weary, remember that God will renew your strength as you place your hope in Him.

"For I know the plans I have for you," declares the Lord, "plans to prosper you and not to harm you, plans to give you hope and a future."

- Jeremiah 29:11

Trust that God has a good plan for your life, filled with hope and a bright future.

For the Spirit God gave us does not make us timid, but gives us power, love, and self-discipline.

- 2 Timothy 1:7

The Holy Spirit gives you power, love, and self-discipline to confidently face challenges.

When Jesus was asked to teach his disciples how to pray, he scripted a prayer to help them pray perfectly to the Father. I believe Jesus was the example we are to follow and that we are empowered by prayers. Therefore, I have taken time to add prayers to this book to help guide you on your journey of empowerment by the Holy Spirit.

A Prayer of Empowerment

Heavenly Father,

We come before you with open hearts and minds, ready to receive your divine power. We acknowledge that our battles are physical and spiritual. And we need your strength and guidance. Lord, we thank you for the gift of the Holy Spirit who dwells within us, equipping us with everything we need to stand firm against the forces of darkness. We ask that you fill us anew with the Holy Spirit's indwelling. We are empowered to fight the good fight of faith. With your help through the empowerment of the Holy Spirit, we have courage and perseverance.

Grant us wisdom to discern the enemy's tactics, faith to extinguish all the flaming arrows of the evil one, and the peace that surpasses all our understanding. Heavenly Father, grow our hearts and empower us.

In the name of Jesus, we pray.

Amen.

A Prayer for the Purpose of this Book

Heavenly Father,

Let the Table of Contents serve as a road map exploring the Holy Spirit's empowerment. Let each chapter build upon the last. Let this book provide a cohesive and comprehensive understanding of how to live a victorious, spirit-enhanced life through and with the Holy Spirit's leading and empowerment.

In the mighty name of Jesus,

Amen!

Chapter 1

My Journey to Empowerment

When I first began my walk with Christ, I often felt overwhelmed by the challenges and spiritual battles I faced. Despite my best efforts, I struggled to live out my faith with the confidence and strength I saw in other believers. It wasn't until I discovered the Holy Spirit and his promises that my journey began to transform. The Holy Spirit's Power is just as vital. It helped me to make wise decisions, transform my character, and equip me to serve others with love and effectiveness.

I encourage you to seek the Holy Spirit's power in your daily life. Pray for His guidance, be open to His leading, and use the gifts He has given you to bless others. By doing so, we can experience the fullness of God's presence and make a meaningful impact in our community and church.

Prayer of Seeking the Holy Spirit in Daily Life

Heavenly Father,

We come before you today with hearts open and eager to experience the fullness of your Holy Spirit. We thank you for the gift of the Holy Spirit, who empowers, guides, Comforts, and transforms us.

Lord, fill us with your power, just as you feel the apostles at the Day of Pentecost. Fill us with boldness to be your witness in our homes. Lord. We also ask for evidence of speaking in tongues as a sign of your Spirit's presence and power.

In Jesus' name,

Amen.

"But you will receive power when the Holy Spirit comes on you, and you will be my witnesses in Jerusalem and in all Judea and Samaria and to the ends of the earth."
- Acts 1:8

The words of Acts deeply resonated with me: You will receive power when the Holy Spirit comes on you. I realized I had been trying to fight my battles with my strength, neglecting the divine power available to me through the Holy Spirit.

I earnestly prayed for the Holy Spirit to fill and empower me that night. I asked God to help me rely not on my abilities but on the Holy Spirit. Over the following weeks and months, I noticed a change in my life. The fear and doubt that once hindered me were replaced with a sense of peace and assurance. I suddenly found myself equipped with wisdom and courage that I had never experienced before. One particular instance stands out. I was facing a difficult situation at work that required tact and strength of character. I felt lacking as I prayed for guidance, but then I felt an overwhelming sense of the Holy Spirit's presence. He gave me the words to speak and the courage to stand firm. The situation was resolved in a way that I could only attribute to God's divine intervention. I know the one thing that I did differently was to allow the Holy Spirit to work in my everyday life. So many times, I can recall times when I tried to figure it out on my own by thinking and rethinking ways to resolve the situation, often feeling lost and bewildered by it. This is so frequently the case. We try to muddle through our circumstances without trusting God with the problem. Perhaps you, too, can imagine some instances in your life where you were at a loss for how to resolve a situation and worried about how circumstances would end up. Had I not trusted the holy spirit and allowed him to empower me even at work, I know things would not have turned out as perfectly as they did for everyone involved Except for the Holy Spirit, empowering me to be a better version of myself. Through this experience, I understood that the promise of the Holy Spirit's empowerment was not just a distant biblical concept but a present practical reality. The Holy Spirit is always ready to empower, guide, and equip us in every moment and is prepared for whatever lies ahead. As you read this book, I pray that you, too, embrace these promises and experience the transformative power of the Holy Spirit in your life. Remember, you are not alone in your struggles. God's Spirit is within you, providing the strength and wisdom to overcome every challenge.

Understanding the Role of the Holy Spirit as the Comforter, Counselor, and Guide

"And I will ask the Father, and he will give you another advocate to help you and be with you forever – the Spirit of truth. The world cannot accept him, because it neither sees him nor knows him. But you know him, for he lives with you and will be in you."
  - John 14:16-17

As our Comforter, the Holy Spirit brings us peace and reassurance, especially during difficulties and uncertainty. This promise from Jesus shares that we are never alone. The Holy Spirit is with us always, providing a sense of divine presence and comfort that the world cannot understand.

Let's Pray!

Heavenly Father,

We come before you with grateful hearts, acknowledging your love and guidance in every step of our journey. Thank you for the gift of the Holy Spirit, who comforts, empowers, and leads us into all truth. Lord, we confess that there have been times when we've tried to walk this journey in our own strength, feeling overwhelmed and unsure. Yet, your Spirit has always been there, waiting to guide us, to fill us with power, and to transform our hearts.

Father, we ask for a fresh outpouring of your Holy Spirit in our lives. Just as you filled the apostles with boldness and power on the Day of Pentecost, fill us now. We open our hearts to receive your Spirit's guidance in every area of our lives—our work, our families, and our daily challenges.

Help us to rely not on our abilities but on the divine strength you've made available through your Spirit.

Lord, empower us to be bold witnesses of your love and truth wherever we are. We ask for the wisdom to face difficult situations with courage and the grace to serve others with love. Let the presence of your Spirit be evident in our lives, transforming our character and equipping us for every good work you've called us to.

We pray for anyone who may be reading this prayer and seeking a deeper relationship with you. Holy Spirit, reveal yourself to them in a powerful way. May they experience your comfort, peace, and strength, knowing that they are never alone.

Thank you, Father, for walking with us every step of the way. Help us to embrace our journey with confidence, trust in your promises, and live for your glory.

In Jesus' name, we pray.

Amen

Reflection

Take a moment to reflect on where you are in your journey with Christ and His Holy Spirit and write it down.

Have you made a fundamental decision to follow Christ and asked the Holy Spirit to empower you in your everyday walk? Can you think of a time when you felt like the Holy Spirit or God's divine intervention was leading you through a situation? Take a few moments to list when you have witnessed God leading through a problem in your life.

Chapter 2

The Promise of the Holy Spirit Empowerment

Exploring Foundations

To expound on the foundations and promises of the Holy Spirit as laid out in the book of Acts, we can begin by understanding the groundwork established and the promises that God made to believers:

At the beginning of the Book of Acts, two foundations were explored. The first was that the Holy Spirit would give divine strength beyond human ability, helping the disciples be empowered to accomplish God's mission for them.

The second foundation that would be established is that this power enabled them to give Holy Spirit-empowered testimonies of the resurrection and deliver the gospel message to the world.

Exploring the Promises

We must first ask ourselves what a promise is. We all know it to be a contract of one's intentions or pledge. Unfortunately, some of us have experienced broken promises. Sometimes, those broken promises are from parents or guardians, and we take that into our experience and believe that God breaks promises, too, as he is our guardian.

Let me assure you that a heavenly promise is different altogether.

Definition of a Promise

A Heavenly promise is a commitment or assurance God gives, grounded in His divine nature and eternal truth. These promises are found in Scripture and reflect God's will, faithfulness, and love toward His people. Unlike earthly promises, which can be broken, Heavenly promises are unwavering and trustworthy because they are rooted in God's perfect character and sovereignty. They often relate to spiritual blessings, eternal life, guidance, provision, and fulfilling His purposes, offering believers hope and assurance in this life and eternity.

PROMISE ONE

"But you will receive power when the Holy Spirit comes on you, and you will be my witnesses in Jerusalem, and in all Judea and Samaria, and to the ends of the earth."

- Acts 1:8

Pentecost (Acts Chapter 2)

This promise states that the Spirit descended on the apostles and other followers of Jesus as tongues of fire. They began speaking in various languages, which enabled them to preach to a diverse crowd in Jerusalem. This event marked the birth of the Christian Church and led to the conversion of about 3000 people.

PROMISE TWO

The Power to speak in tongues was not only about reaching people of diverse tongues and allowing believers to talk privately with their Heavenly Father, a perfect spiritual and divine prayer that no enemy could interpret.

It is one of the most beautiful promises of the Holy Spirit, and His role is to help us communicate with God, especially when we're struggling to find the right words. In Romans 8:26-27, we learn that the Spirit comes alongside us in our weakness. When we don't even know how to pray, the Holy Spirit steps in, interceding for us in ways that go beyond words—almost like a divine translator who understands our hearts even better than we do. He speaks directly to God on our behalf, making sure that our unspoken needs and desires are known.

Another powerful reminder of this promise is found in Ephesians 2:18, where we're told that through Jesus, we have direct access to God the Father by the Holy Spirit. This means that even in the most private and intimate moments, when we may feel inadequate or unsure, the Holy Spirit ensures that our prayers reach the Father.

One of the Holy Spirit's incredible promises is that we don't have to rely on perfect words or flawless prayers. Even in silence or confusion, the Spirit is there, helping us connect with God profoundly and personally.

PROMISE THREE

The third beautiful promise of the Holy Spirit is that He empowers us to proclaim the truth about Jesus boldly. One of the most striking examples is in Peter's message at Pentecost. Just imagine the scene: a crowd of people from all over, each speaking different languages, gathered in Jerusalem. Suddenly, the apostles, ordinary men, began speaking in the native tongues of these visitors, a miracle made possible by the Holy Spirit. People were amazed, confused, and some even skeptical, thinking the apostles had been drinking.

But then Peter, filled with the Holy Spirit, stood up and delivered a powerful message that would change everything. He explained that what they were witnessing was the fulfillment of an ancient promise from God. Quoting the prophet Joel, Peter told them that God had promised to pour out His Spirit on all people, and this miraculous moment was proof that the time had come.

Peter's message wasn't just about the miracle they had seen. It was about Jesus—the one they had crucified but who had risen from the dead. With boldness and clarity, Peter proclaimed that Jesus was the Messiah they had been waiting for. He reminded them that although they had rejected Him, this had all been part of God's plan to bring salvation to the world.

And here's where the third promise of the Holy Spirit comes in: the same Spirit who had empowered Peter to speak so boldly was now being offered to everyone. Peter called the people to repent, to turn from their sins, and to be baptized in the name of Jesus for the forgiveness of their sins. And in return, they, too, would receive the gift of the Holy Spirit.

This promise is just as true for us today as it was then. The Holy Spirit gives us the courage and the words to speak the truth about Jesus, even when we feel unqualified or afraid. Just like Peter, who had once denied Jesus out of fear, we can be transformed by the Spirit to stand boldly for Christ. The Holy Spirit empowers us to share the good news in a way that reaches hearts and changes lives—just like it did for the 3,000 people who came to faith that day.

So, the third promise of the Holy Spirit is this: He gives us the boldness to proclaim Jesus as Lord, and through us, He draws others into God's life-changing love. Peter's Message: Filled with the Holy Spirit, Peter delivered a powerful message explaining the significance of Pentecost and proclaiming Jesus Christ as the Messiah. His message, inspired by the Holy Spirit, led to many conversions.

PROMISE FOUR

Healing and Miracles

The fourth promise of the Holy Spirit is His power to bring healing and miracles into our lives. In the early days of the Church, the apostles performed many incredible signs and wonders through the power of the Holy Spirit, and one of the most beautiful examples is the story of Peter and John at the temple gate called Beautiful.

There, they encountered a man who had been lame since birth. Every day, he sat at the gate, asking for money from those passing by. But Peter and John had something far more valuable to offer him. Peter looked at the man and said, "Silver or gold I do not have, but what I do have, I give you. In the name of Jesus Christ of Nazareth, walk." And in that moment, the man was healed through the power of the Holy Spirit. He didn't just stand—he jumped to his feet, walking and praising God for what had happened.

This miraculous healing didn't just change the man's life; it became a powerful testimony to everyone who witnessed it. Crowds gathered, amazed at what they had seen, and many more people came to believe in Jesus because of this miracle.

The Holy Spirit's power wasn't just for the apostles or for that moment in time—it's a promise that still applies to us today. He brings healing, both physically and spiritually, and works through us to touch the lives of those around us. Whether through a miraculous event or the quiet transformation of a person's heart, the Spirit is actively working to make the message of Jesus known.

So, the fourth promise of the Holy Spirit is His ability to bring healing and perform miracles in our lives and the lives of others. His power isn't limited to the extraordinary but also works in the everyday moments, guiding, transforming, and empowering us to be vessels of God's love and grace in a world that desperately needs it.

Let's Pray!

Empowerment Prayer

Heavenly Father,

We come before you with hearts full of gratitude for the incredible promises you have made to us through your Holy Spirit. Thank you for the assurance that we are never alone on this journey. As we explore the foundations of the Holy Spirit's empowerment, we recognize our need for your divine strength beyond our own abilities. Empower us to fulfill the mission you've called us to, just as you empowered the early disciples.

Lord, help us to grasp the depth of your heavenly promises. Remind us that your promises are steadfast and unbreakable, rooted in your perfect character. Teach us to trust in your faithfulness, especially when we face challenges that make us question our worth or your plans for us. May we always remember that your Spirit intercedes for us, even when we struggle to find the right words.

We pray for the boldness to proclaim the truth of Jesus Christ, just as Peter did on the day of Pentecost. Fill us with the Holy Spirit so that we may speak with clarity and courage, drawing others into your love and grace. Help us to be instruments of healing and miracles in our communities, sharing the hope we find in you.

As we embrace the promises of the Holy Spirit, may we experience transformation in our lives and witness the miraculous power of your Spirit at work. We ask that you open our eyes to see the opportunities around us to serve others and to share the good news of Jesus Christ.

Thank you, Father, for the gift of the Holy Spirit and the empowering presence that guides us daily. May our lives reflect your glory as we walk in faith and trust in your promises.

In Jesus' name, we pray.

Amen

Reflection

Each of us comes from a different starting point and reference point with God. If you read this book, I believe you are searching for God's empowerment in your life. You want the Holy Spirit to lead you and empower you to know and do all God has intended for you in your journey. Sometimes, you must reflect on where you have been to see where you are going. Therefore, we must all consider our own experiences and the places they have taken us.

Your Personal Experience with the Holy Spirit

Can you reflect on a time when you have witnessed Christ working through the promises of the Holy Spirit, either in your life or someone else?

Can you recall any essential or minor decisions you have made where you feel the Holy Spirit may have led you?

How has the Holy Spirit guided you in making important decisions?

In the Bible, the disciples were given the ability to speak in a heavenly language, often called speaking in tongues. The Bible says that God is the same yesterday, today, and forever, which means that the miracles we saw in the first church are possible today. Hebrews 13:8 says, *"Jesus Christ is the same yesterday and today and forever."* This verse emphasizes the unchanging nature of Jesus Christ, affirming His consistency and reliability across all times.

Have you ever experienced speaking in tongues? If so, can you share what the experience was like for you? If not, have you ever witnessed others speaking in tongues during a worship service? How did it impact you? And why?

If you want to receive the baptism of the Holy Spirit with the evidence of speaking in tongues, pray about and seek guidance through joining a Full Gospel, Assemblies of God, or Pentecostal church.

Chapter 3

Holy Spirit's Role: Comforter, Counselor, Guide

Comforter

In my own life, I have experienced—the comforting presence of the Holy Spirit during some of the most challenging moments. There were times when I felt overwhelmed by grief after losing a loved one.

In those dark moments, I prayed and asked the Holy Spirit to comfort me, and when I gave my sorrow to him, I felt a profound sense of peace. That could only come from the Holy Spirit. It was as if a warm embrace surrounded me, reminding me that God was with me and that I was not alone in my sorrow.

This comfort gave me the strength to move forward and to trust in God's plan, even when it was hard to see. Loss is a part of life that we often feel unprepared for. So many times, loss can even come as a surprise. God gives a promise in scripture that we can stand on.

When we face seasons of deep sorrow and loss, one of the most beautiful promises we can hold onto is that the Holy Spirit is our Comforter. In the Beatitudes, Jesus says in Matthew 5:4, *"Blessed are those who mourn, for they will be comforted."* It's such a simple yet profound truth: God's comfort is promised to us when we mourn. It doesn't mean the pain disappears overnight, but it assures us that we're not alone in our grief. The Holy Spirit is right there with us, offering peace that goes beyond what we can understand.

Another scripture that speaks to this is Psalm 34:18. *"The Lord is close to the brokenhearted and saves those who are crushed in spirit."* This passage reminds us that God draws especially near to us when we're hurting. In those moments when our hearts feel shattered, the Holy Spirit is present, bringing comfort and healing to our souls.

Grief is never easy, but the Holy Spirit doesn't leave us to walk through it alone. Whether it's through quiet moments of peace, the encouragement of others, or simply knowing that God is close, the Spirit comes alongside us in our mourning. He's there to comfort us, to lift us up, and to remind us that even in our darkest hours, we are deeply loved and cared for.

Counselor

Remember that I talked about my career struggle and how the Holy Spirit worked it out? The decision was critical to my career path. I was at a crossroads in my life, uncertain about which direction to take, and felt the weight of the choice pressing on me.

Through prayer and seeking the Holy Spirit's guidance, I experienced the Holy Spirit as my Councilor. The Holy Spirit brought specific scriptures to my mind, providing insight I hadn't considered before. This divine guidance led me to make a decision aligned with God's will for my life, and it brought about blessings I couldn't have anticipated.

It is essential for you to spend time in God's word. Through the study of God's word, you, the Holy Spirit, can guide you to God's perfect will for your life. One fundamental scripture to remember is John 14:26 (NIV), *"But the Advocate, the Holy Spirit, whom the Father will send in my name, will teach you all the things and will remind you of everything I have said to you."*

Guide

We all face transitional times in our lives, times when we are switching chapters and embarking on something new, which can be a little scary and unsure.

The Holy Spirit's guidance has been invaluable to me. One particular instance stands out to me. I was uncertain about a major life transition that involved moving to a new city and starting a new ministry. I prayed frequently for directions. The Holy Spirit moved in a new way. I began to find my direction by paying attention to what opportunities opened up and gave me peace. Doors began to open, and I was provided confirmation through circumstances. I also received confirmation through the council of spirit-filled believers. His clear and undeniable guidance led me to step out in faith. My reliance on the Holy Spirit during this move represented a breakthrough in my spiritual growth and in ministry, demon-

strating the importance of the Holy Spirit's guidance in fulfilling God's promises for my life.

These scriptures and personal experiences illustrate the
vital roles of the Holy Spirit in our lives as believers. We can
draw Immense strength and encouragement from knowing
that the Holy Spirit is our Comforter and counselor. Searching out God, embracing His presence, and seeking His guidance daily will empower us to live victoriously and faithfully
in our walk with Him as Guide.

*"But when he, the Spirit of truth, comes, he will guide you into all
the truth. He will not speak on his own; he will speak only what
he hears, and he will tell you what is yet to come."*
   - John 16:13

Let's Pray!

Heavenly Father,

We come before you today with grateful hearts, acknowledging the incredible gift of the Holy Spirit in our lives.
Thank you for sending your Spirit to be our Comforter,
Counselor, and Guide. In our times of sorrow and loss, we
are reminded of your promise that the Holy Spirit will be
with us, providing comfort and peace that surpasses all understanding.

Lord, we thank you for the moments when we have felt
overwhelmed by grief and heartache. Just as you promised,
your Holy Spirit has embraced us in our darkest times, reminding us that we are never alone. May those who are
mourning today feel your presence surrounding them, bringing healing and solace to their hearts. Help us to lean into

your comfort, knowing that our pain is understood and held in your loving arms.

As we navigate the complexities of life, we ask for the Holy Spirit's counsel in our decisions. Grant us wisdom and discernment, just as you have done for those who have come before us. Help us to immerse ourselves in your Word, allowing the Holy Spirit to illuminate our path and guide us toward your perfect will. May we always seek your direction in every choice we face, trusting that your plans for us are good and filled with hope.

Lord, as we embark on new chapters and transitions, may we remain sensitive to the Holy Spirit's leading. Open our eyes to the opportunities you place before us and give us the courage to step out in faith. We trust that your Spirit will guide us into all truth, helping us navigate the uncertainties of life with confidence and grace.

Thank you, Father, for the Holy Spirit, our divine Comforter, Counselor, and Guide. Help us to cultivate a deeper relationship with Him, embracing His presence in every moment. May we walk boldly in your promises, empowered by your Spirit to live out our calling and share your love with the world.

In Jesus' name, we pray.

Amen

Reflection

Holy Spirit as Comforter

Can you think of a time in your life when you experienced grief or loss? How did you respond in that season, and did you feel the comforting presence of the Holy Spirit?

In your moments of mourning, how can you actively invite the Holy Spirit to bring you comfort and peace?

Matthew 5:4 tells us, *"Blessed are those who mourn, for they will be comforted."* What does this promise mean to you personally in times of sorrow? How does it shape your understanding of God's care for you during challenging times?

Holy Spirit as Counselor

Have you ever faced a crossroads, like a significant decision or challenge, and sought guidance from the Holy Spirit? What was that experience like for you?

How does the Holy Spirit speak to you personally—through scripture, prayer, circumstances, or other ways? What practical steps can you take to listen more closely to His guidance?

In John 14:26, Jesus promised that the Holy Spirit would teach and remind us of all He has said. How has the Holy Spirit brought clarity or direction to your life through God's Word?

Holy Spirit as Guide

Think about a time when you were facing a significant life transition. How did you seek the Holy Spirit's guidance? In what ways did you see God confirming His direction for you?

How can you become more attuned to the Holy Spirit's guidance in your everyday decisions and actions?

What does it look like to fully trust His leading, even when the path seems unclear or challenging?

John 16:13 promises that the Holy Spirit will guide us into all truth. How does this truth bring you comfort, and how can you lean on it more in uncertain or transitional moments?

Applying the Holy Spirit's Role to Your Life

In what area of your life do you most need the Holy Spirit's comfort, counsel, or guidance right now? How can you invite Him into that situation?

How might your spiritual growth be deepened if you consistently relied on the Holy Spirit as your Comforter, Counselor, and Guide? What steps can you take to strengthen your relationship with Him in these roles?

Chapter 4

Spiritual Weapons and Armor

Equipping Yourself for Spiritual Warfare

What is spiritual warfare in the practical sense?

I do not know about you, but I think of epic battles between heroic angels and dark demonic demons when I think of spiritual warfare. The Bible says that spiritual warfare refers to the ongoing struggle between good and evil in the darkness, in the spiritual realm. It is a concept rooted in the belief that there are spiritual forces at work in the world, both angelic (good) and demonic (evil), Engaged in a conflict that affects individuals, communities, and nations. All that sounds overwhelming and clinical. The spiritual battle in its most practical form can be as simple as that meme of an angel sitting on one shoulder telling you to do good and a demon on the other telling you to make the wrong choice.

Finally, be strong in the Lord and in his mighty power. Put on the full armor of God, so that you can take your stand against the devil's schemes.

- Ephesians 6:10-11

It is essential to realize that we are involved in spiritual warfare daily, which can take many forms. Spiritual warfare doesn't always involve dramatic battles or supernatural encounters. For most Christians, it's far more subtle and often takes place in ordinary moments of life. It's important to recognize how these spiritual struggles can surface so we can stand firm in faith and be equipped with God's armor.

The Battle Within

One of the most common forms of spiritual warfare happens within ourselves—our thoughts, desires, and emotions. We all face temptation in some form, whether it's the lure of pride, lust, or greed. These moments can feel like a tug-of-war between what we know is right and the urges pulling us in the opposite direction. It's not just about resisting temptation but recognizing that every battle we face in these moments is a spiritual one.

Then there's the struggle with doubt and fear—those times when we question if God really is good or if He's really listening. When fear about the future takes over, it can feel like a spiritual weight on our shoulders. Anxiety, depression, and hopelessness can also be part of this inner struggle. These aren't just emotional battles—they're spiritual ones, seeking to pull us away from our hope in Christ.

Conflict in Our Relationships

We also see spiritual warfare at work in our relationships. Whether it's tension in our families, misunderstandings with friends, or divisions in our churches, these conflicts often go deeper than what's on the surface. The enemy wants to sow discord and division because he knows that unity among believers is powerful. When we're arguing, holding grudges, or withholding forgiveness, we may unknowingly be engaging in a spiritual battle.

Facing Challenges in the World Around Us

The world we live in presents its own forms of spiritual warfare. We're constantly surrounded by distractions—things that pull our focus away from God. Whether it's the relentless busyness of life or the constant noise of social media and entertainment, it's easy to neglect time with God. We might even become spiritually complacent, losing that sense of urgency or passion in our faith. This, too, is part of the battle—keeping our hearts aligned with God when the world is constantly pulling us in other directions.

In our workplaces or public life, we might feel pressure to compromise our values. Maybe we're asked to cut corners or engage in behavior that conflicts with our Christian beliefs. Sometimes, it's the feeling of isolation—being the only believer in a secular environment where faith is unwelcome or even mocked. These are the subtle but real ways we're drawn into spiritual warfare daily.

The Subtle Deceptions

Another form of warfare we often miss is deception. Whether it's a false teaching that leads us away from biblical truth or the influence of a culture that contradicts God's Word, we can easily be led astray. These deceptions might seem harmless initially, but they chip away at our foundation of faith over time.

Oppression and Spiritual Attacks

While not as common for every believer, some experience more direct spiritual attacks—oppression from dark forces. This can come in the form of recurring negative thoughts, overwhelming fear, or even strange occurrences that feel demonic in nature. It's a reminder that the spiritual realm is very real, and sometimes, the battle takes on a form that we can't explain with natural reasoning.

The Attack on Our Prayer Life

Perhaps one of the most telling signs of spiritual warfare is when our prayer life begins to falter. Distractions during prayer, an overwhelming sense of busyness, or even an unusual disinterest in spending time with God can be tactics used to weaken our connection with Him. The enemy knows that when we stop praying, we stop drawing from our source of strength.

Standing Firm

In all of these battles, it's clear that spiritual warfare is not just about external forces or dramatic moments. It's our everyday struggles—the pull toward temptation, the doubts that creep in, the conflicts that arise, and the distractions that take our focus off God. But the good news is, we don't face these battles alone. God equips us with spiritual armor for a reason: because He knows the battles are real and constant.

By staying rooted in prayer, holding onto the truth of Scripture, and standing firm in our faith, we can resist the enemy's schemes and find victory even in the midst of the struggles.

Spiritual warfare involves the struggle against sin, temptation, and the influence of demonic forces that seek to oppose God's promises and hinder believers in their walk of faith. It encompasses various forms of spiritual attacks, such as temptations, deceptions, obsessions, and even confrontation with demonic entities.

Believers engage in and conquer spiritual warfare through daily steps, which I like to remind myself of with affirmations. Here are two examples.

Prayer and Intercession

I seek God's intervention and protection by reading scripture and learning the truth. I use God's Word to counter lies and deceit. I build faith and trust by studying scripture and taking it to heart because I rely on God's strength and promises.

Spiritual Discernment

I recognize spiritual attacks and resist them.

Jesus Christ conquered sin and death through his death and resurrection, and He alone is credited with the ultimate victory in spiritual warfare. As a believer, I am called, and you, as believers, are called to stand firm in faith and be equipped with spiritual armor.

Finally, I will be strong In the Lord and in His mighty power; I put on the whole armor of God to stand against the devil's schemes, for I recognize that our struggle is not against flesh and blood but against the rulers, against authorities, against the powers of this dark world, and the spiritual forces of evil in the heavenly realms. Therefore, I put on the whole armor of God so that when the day of evil comes, I may be able to stand my ground and have done everything to stand. Therefore, I stand firm then, with the belt of truth buckled around my waist, the breastplate of righteousness in place, and my feet fitted with the redness. They come from the gospel of peace. In addition to all this, I take up the shield of faith, with which I can extinguish all the flaming arrows of the evil one. I wear the helmet of salvation, carry the sword of the Spirit, which is the Word of God, and pray in the Spirit on all occasions with all kinds of prayers and requests. I stand on scripture, which is the word of God. Ephesians chapter 6:10 -18 empowered by the Holy Spirit to overcome the forces of darkness.

I suggest you learn these affirmations and study to help you remember who you are in your spiritual battle.

Understanding spiritual warfare is crucial for believers to live victoriously and fulfill their God-given purpose. Their God-given purpose relies on God's power and protection in the face of challenges in this world, **both physical and spiritual**.

I have faced a lot of spiritual warfare in all areas of my life. Let's face it; most of us spend a lot of time at work, and it can be as taxing as any place else to deal with spiritual warfare. Spiritual warfare in the workplace can indeed be challenging and unsettling. It is the one place where many of us spend a lot of time. It can manifest in various forms, such as conflicts with coworkers, Ethical dilemmas, temptation to compromise values, and even feeling spiritually drained amidst a hostile environment. Wherever you experience your spiritual challenges, whether in the workplace, in your home, or wherever the enemy chooses to attack you, you can be sure that the Lord is there to guide and defend you through understanding His word and how it applies to you. We must be fully immersed in our faith in the words of the Lord's word, and he will raise a standard to protect and preserve us through the power of the Holy Spirit working actively in our lives. I promise you one thing: it all begins with prayer.

Let's pray!

Prayer for Spiritual Warfare

Dear Heavenly Father,

I come before you, acknowledging that I engage in spiritual warfare in my daily walk with you, Lord, whether in my workplace or any place where I spend my time. Lord, I ask for your divine protection and guidance as I navigate challenges and conflicts. Cloth me with your spiritual armor, the belt of truth, the breastplate of righteousness, the shoes of peace, the shield of faith, the helmet of salvation, and the sword of the Spirit. Fill me afresh with your Holy Spirit, empowering me to stand firm against every scene of the enemy. Help me maintain integrity, speak with wisdom and grace, and reflect your love and all I do, God, my heart and mind from negativity and discouragement. And grant me discernment to recognize spiritual attacks. Lord, I trust in your promises that no weapon formed against me shall prosper. Strengthen my faith in renewing my strength each day, and make my life glorify you. May your light shine through me in my home, workplace, and every place I witness.

In Jesus' name.

Amen

Reflection

How do you personally experience spiritual warfare in your life, and how does Ephesians 6:10-18 shape your understanding of it?

Which piece of God's armor do you find most essential in your current spiritual battles, and which area do you need to strengthen?

How do you discern spiritual attacks, and what practical steps can you take to resist them using prayer and God's Word?

How does your faith in God's power and protection influence your response to challenges, especially in the workplace or other areas of life?

How can you invite the Holy Spirit to empower you to stand firm and overcome the enemy's schemes in your daily walk?

Chapter 5

Walking in Your Spiritual Authority

Exercising Authority in Christ

"I have given you authority to trample on snakes and scorpions and to overcome all the power of the enemy; nothing will harm you."

    - Luke 10:19

This verse assures believers that through the authority given by Jesus, they have the power to overcome their enemy's schemes and attacks. It emphasizes that God wants to protect us. It shows the authority God grants us and reinforces the promise that, as believers, we have the right to exercise the authority of Christ in our everyday lives. We can trust in God's protection and provision, knowing that, ultimately, nothing can harm our eternal souls. This scripture assures us that the Holy Spirit is a source of strength and confidence for believers. We all navigate spiritual battles and physical challenges in our lives. We can be confident that by leaning into the Holy Spirit, learning the truth of the Bible, and being fully convinced of our faith, we have the power to trample on evil of all kinds.

Jesus' words to his disciples empower them with authority over spiritual forces, assuring them of heavenly protection from harm. It underscores the believer's authority in Christ. Knowing that God is behind us to guide and comfort us and enable us to overcome spiritual challenges and adversities

Taking Authority for Myself and My Family

Looking further at Luke 10:19, Jesus is speaking to His disciples, granting them authority over spiritual forces of evil. The "serpents and scorpions" symbolize demonic powers and any evil plans of Satan against you. Jesus reassures believers of their protection and authority over the enemy's schemes. This fits well into the context of spiritual warfare, reminding us that God equips His followers with power to overcome the enemy.

This revelation became a cornerstone for me. Luke 10:19 reassured me that I was not powerless against these attacks.

There was a time in my life when I faced overwhelming challenges—every day. I felt spiritually attacked and emotionally drained. My family also felt the effects of this battle as the stress and negativity began to impact our home life. I knew I had to take a stand and exercise God's authority. I started to immerse myself in prayer through the name of Jesus Christ for myself and my family. I was seeking God's guidance and strength. I meditated daily on the scriptures that spoke of our authority given through the power of the Holy Spirit. I have spiritual authority in Christ and the protection He provides through His promises. Through prayer, I declared God's promises and rebuked any spiritual forces that sought to undermine us as individuals or as a family. I constantly spoke life and truth over our home and family, trusting God's power to protect and guide us.

Another great story of spiritual authority is that of David and Goliath.

Taking Spiritual Authority: David and Goliath

The story of David and Goliath is one of the most famous tales in the Bible, and for good reason. It speaks to the heart and shows us what it means to take spiritual authority, even when everything seems stacked against us.

THE SETTING

Picture this: the Israelites and the Philistines are camped on opposite sides of a valley, ready for battle. For forty days, the Philistine giant Goliath has taunted the Israelites, challenging them to send out a champion to fight him. He's massive, towering over everyone, and his intimidating presence has paralyzed the Israelite army with fear.

DAVID'S ENTRANCE

Now, enter David—a young shepherd boy delivering food to his brothers in the army. When David hears Goliath's insults, something stirs within him. Instead of feeling fear, he feels a surge of righteous anger. To him, this isn't just a personal challenge; it's an affront to God.

CLAIMING AUTHORITY

David steps forward and tells King Saul, "Don't worry; I'll fight this giant!" His confidence surprises everyone. David recounts how he's fought off lions and bears while protecting his sheep, attributing his courage to God's help. It's clear David sees the battle not just as a physical confrontation but as a **spiritual one.**

When David faces Goliath, he doesn't wear armor or carry a sword. Instead, he picks up five smooth stones from a nearby stream. As he approaches the giant, Goliath mocks him, but David doesn't back down. He declares, "You come with weapons, but I come in the name of the Lord."

THE VICTORY

With one swift motion, David slings a stone that hits Goliath squarely in the forehead, and the giant falls. The Israelites, once paralyzed by fear, now erupt in cheers as they witness this incredible victory. David's courage has not only defeated Goliath but has also inspired an entire nation.

THE LESSON

David's story teaches us a powerful lesson about exercising spiritual authority. It reminds us that, like David, we all face giants in our lives—challenges that seem overwhelming. But when we stand firm in our faith and trust in God's strength, we can overcome even the biggest obstacles.

In our moments of doubt or fear, we can look to David's example. We don't have to feel equipped or powerful alone; we must remember that God is with us. When we lean on Him, we can find the courage to face our giants and claim the victories waiting for us.

Here are some of the promises that I routinely speak when I am in a battle.

Belonging to God

"You, dear children, are from God and have overcome them, because the one who is in you is greater than the one who is in the world."
  - 1 John 4:4

This scripture affirms that we are God's children. Our identity is rooted in Him, who gives us a sense of belonging and security.

Victory Through Christ

And they overcame him by the blood of the Lamb, and by the word of their testimony; and they loved not their lives unto the death.
  - Revelation 12:11 (KJV)

This scripture tells us that through Christ, we have already overcome the challenges and adversaries of this world.

Our victory is assured because of our faith in Him.

Behold, I give unto you power to tread on serpents and scorpions, and over all the power of the enemy: and nothing shall by any means hurt you.
  - Luke 10:19 (KJV)

I can do all this through him who gives me strength.
  - Philippians 4:13

With Christ in me, I am equipped to face any challenge with confidence, knowing that His strength and power are at work within me. No matter the adversity or opposition, I am more than a conqueror through Him who loves me. Amen!

As I exercise this Authority, I notice a change. God began to shift. The atmosphere and I felt a renewed sense of peace and confidence.

How can I encourage you? **Biblical Truth**. Immerse yourself in Scripture. Know the Word of God and the promises He has given you.

Read Scriptures

Luke 10:19

Romans, chapters 8 and 37

1 John 4:4

Affirm your authority, and victory will come. We have Christ. Meditate regularly on these verses to strengthen your faith.

Pray with Authority

Approach prayer with confidence. Knowing that you have Christ's authority, declare God's promises over your life, family, and situation. Speak against any spiritual opposition and trust that God hears and acts on your prayers.

Stay Close to God

Cultivate a deep relationship with God through regular prayer. Worship and Bible study. The closer you ought to God, the more confidence you will have in His power and protection

Final Assurance

You are not alone in this journey. Just as I experienced victory through taking authority in Christ, you two can walk in boldness and assurance, knowing that nothing can ultimately harm you when you are in God's hands. Walking in God-given authority means trusting God is with you and for you. Do not let fear hold you back. Stand firm in your faith.

Remember God's Faithfulness

Reflect on past experiences where God has come through for you. Remembering His faithfulness can bolster your confidence in His ability to protect. Empower you now.

Let's Pray!

Let's believe God. He will move mightily in your situation.

Heavenly Father,

I come before you with a heart full of faith and confidence in your mighty power. Your words tell me that you have given me authority over all the power of the enemy and that nothing shall by any means hurt me. You remind me that I can do everything through Christ, who strengthens me. Today, I stand on your promises. Lord, I declare that greater is he who is in me than in the world. No weapon formed against me shall prosper, and I shall condemn every tongue that rises against me in judgment (Isaiah 54:17). I ask for your strength and Courage to face every challenge that comes my way. I hoped you could fill me with your Holy Spirit, empowering me to stand firm. My faith and ability to overcome every obstacle grant me wisdom, discernment, and peace that suppresses all understanding. Lord, I trust in your unfailing love and faithfulness. I surrender my fears and doubts to you. And I embraced the victory that is minds through Jesus Christ. Thank you for your constant presence and for the power that works within me.

In Jesus' mighty name, I pray.

Amen

Let's touch spiritually and agree in prayer, knowing God's power is at work among us.

Heavenly Father,

We come before you with a grateful heart, acknowledging your greatness and the authority you have given us through your son Jesus Christ, Lord. We thank you for the victory that has been warned on the cross and the power of the holy spirit that dwells within us. Father, we lift every believer to you, asking that you open their eyes to the authority they possess in Christ. May they recognize that they are more than conquerors through Him who loved us and that they can trample over snakes and scorpions and overcome all the power of the enemy.

Thank you, Lord, for the authority you have given us and for the assurance of your protection and guidance. Help us all to live out this authority with courage and faith, bringing glory to your name. May this prayer inspire and encourage you to step into the authority given.to them by Christ, and may they walk in victory and confidence, knowing that the Holy Spirit empowers them

In Jesus' mighty name, we pray.

Amen

Reflection

Understanding Your Authority in Christ

Reflect on Luke 10:19, where Jesus gives His followers authority over the enemy. What does it mean for you personally to have this authority?

How does knowing that nothing can harm you in a spiritual sense give you confidence as a believer?

Consider moments when you felt powerless. How could embracing this authority change your perspective?

Overcoming Spiritual Challenges

Think about the battles you face, whether spiritual, emotional, or relational. How can you apply the authority Jesus gave you in these situations?

How does this authority empower you to confront fear, temptation, or spiritual oppression?

Reflect on specific challenges where you need to declare your authority in Christ and trust in His victory.

Speaking Life Over Your Family and Loved Ones

Just as you took authority for yourself and your family, reflect on how to extend that spiritual protection to others. How can you declare God's promises and pray with authority over your loved ones?

Consider ways to invite God's peace, protection, and power into your home and relationships through intentional prayer and Scripture.

Praying with Authority

Reflect on the difference between praying out of fear and praying with confidence in the authority Christ has given you. How can you shift your prayer life to align with this divine authority?

Consider how praying with boldness, rooted in Scripture and faith, can transform your spiritual walk and bring about breakthroughs in areas where you've felt resistance.

Chapter 6

Empowerment in Action: Lessons from Scripture

The Bible is full of stories where God empowers ordinary individuals to fulfill extraordinary purposes. These examples remind us that God equips those He calls, no matter their fears or feelings of inadequacy. Below are some inspiring stories of biblical empowerment that show us how God's strength is made perfect in our weakness.

The Story of Moses' Empowerment

Moses: Empowered to Lead

Exodus, chapters 3-4

Moses' journey of empowerment started at the burning bush. God assured him of His presence despite his doubts and fears, giving Moses the strength and signs to confront Pharaoh and lead the Israelites out of Egypt. Moses didn't feel qualified—he questioned his speech, abilities, and even God's choice. Yet, God empowered him to fulfill a destiny that seemed far beyond his capabilities.

Moses' story shows us that God can use us powerfully, even when we feel incapable. His strength shines through our weaknesses.

Applying Moses' Experience to Our Lives

Like Moses, we all face moments when we feel unqualified, uncertain, or fearful about stepping into what God calls us to do. These moments, however, are often where God meets us, ready to empower us just as He did for Moses.

Recognizing God's Calling

Like Moses, we are called to specific purposes, big or small. Even when we feel overwhelmed or inadequate, God calls us with His empowerment, not our own strength. Trusting in His presence gives us the courage to move forward.

Acknowledging My Doubts

It's natural to doubt, just as Moses did. In my own journey, I've faced doubts and challenges, especially in my career. Sometimes, I felt like my abilities were being questioned, and I began questioning myself. During those tough times, I leaned into God's promises. Just as He reassured Moses, He reassured me that He was with me.

I found strength beyond human understanding, allowing me to persevere even when the situation seemed impossible. Moses experienced the same divine empowerment. God's presence gave me the strength to stand firm amidst negativity and criticism.

Have you ever faced doubt or opposition in your life, personally or professionally? How did you handle those moments? I would love to hear your stories. Sometimes, sharing these experiences can remind us that we're not alone in our struggles and that God is working through them.

Let's Pray!

Heavenly Father,

As we come before you today, we remember how you strengthened and powered Moses despite his doubts and fears. Just as you assured Moses of your presence and gave him the courage to face great challenges, we asked for the same strength and reassurance in our lives. Lord, I pray for each person reading this book to overcome any doubt or fear that may be experienced and fill us with the confidence that comes from knowing you are with us just as you were with Moses. Help us trust in your guidance and step forward with faith. Grant us your peace and courage to face our obstacles with the assurance that your power within us is greater than any fear or opposition. Strengthen our hearts and minds and remind us of your constant peace and support.

We pray this in the name of Jesus, who empowers us as you empowered Moses.

Amen

The Story of Joshua's Empowerment

Joshua Empowered with Courage

Joshua 1:1-9

After Moses' death, Joshua was commissioned to lead the Israelites into the Promised Land. God repeatedly told Joshua to be strong and courageous, promising to be with him as he was with Moses. Joshua's Godly leadership and strength in military victories testified to God's empowering presence, reminding us that courage stems from trusting God's presence.

Empowered to be Courageous

"Have I not commanded you? Be strong and courageous. Do not be afraid; do not be discouraged, for the Lord your God will be with you wherever you go."
    - Joshua 1:9

God gives Joshua a direct command as he prepares to lead the Israelites into the Promised Land. This command is not just a call to physical strength but an assurance of God's presence. God knows the challenges Joshua will face and provides both a directive and a promise.

In the same way, God is aware of what you and I face throughout each day. He knows our struggles, our doubts, and our fears, yet He assures us of His constant presence and support. Just as He was with Moses and Joshua, He is with us every step of the way—commanding us to be strong.

God commanded Joshua to be strong and courageous, indicating that strength and courage are not merely personal qualities but are empowered by the divine command and the presence of God working in our lives.

The promise that the Lord your God is with you wherever you go reassures us that God's presence accompanies us throughout every challenge and transaction.

Life Application

Remember that no matter what challenges arise, you are not alone.

God's guidance and support are with us throughout it all.

God's Ever-present Support

I know that there are times that you feel alone; it is the human condition to feel alone at times. We have all experienced it, and I am sure we wondered what to do in those circumstances. There were times when I felt utterly alone, as though God was distant and not present. In my struggles, I faced moments of doubt and despair, wondering if it was supported or guided. During these times, it was easy to feel isolated and question whether God was with me. Looking back, I can see that God was there with me all along, even when I couldn't feel His presence. He was providing strength, comfort, and guidance, just as God assured Joshua.

The Lord your God is with you wherever you go. I realize now that His presence was constant in my life. His support was there even when I couldn't see it or feel it. He guided me through my challenges and prepared me for what was ahead. Through reflection and prayer, I've understood that God's presence isn't always immediately felt but is always real and dependable. He walks with us through every trial and triumph, even when we may not know it. I shared this testimony to encourage anyone feeling alone or questioning God's presence in their life. Remember that God's assurance to be with us remains true regardless of our circumstances. God's support is unwavering, and He is with us every step of the way.

Let's Pray!

A Prayer of Protection and Reassurance

Heavenly Father,

I come before you with a heart full of gratitude, acknowledging your unwavering presence and power in my life. Just as you empowered Joshua with strength and courage to lead the Israelites, I ask that you empower me in the same way. When challenges feel overwhelming and doubt creeps in, remind me that you are with me, guiding and supporting me through every step.

Lord, I ask for the courage to face the unknown, the strength to persevere through difficult times, and the faith to trust in your constant presence. Just as you promised Joshua that you would be with him wherever he went, I hold onto that promise in my life. Help me be strong and courageous, not relying on my abilities but leaning fully on your strength and wisdom.

When I feel alone or unsure, fill me with the assurance that you are walking with me, even when I can't see it. Teach me to trust in your faithfulness, knowing that you never leave or forsake me. Strengthen me, Lord, to rise up with confidence in your promises, to stand firm in my faith, and to boldly walk the path you have set before me.

Thank you for being my guide, protector, and source of courage. I trust in your empowering presence to lead me through every trial and triumph, just as you did with Joshua.

In Jesus' name, I pray.

Amen

Let me assure you that God is only a breath away. You are not alone; you only need to call on Him, and He will be there.

Heavenly Father,

We come before you with hearts full of faith, asking for your protection against the enemy's schemes. Your word tells us that the enemy comes to steal, kill, and destroy. (John 10:10), But we trust in your promise to Guard us from harm.

Lord, we know that we are never alone. You promised to be with us even in the darkest times. Just as you're sure, Joshua, of your presence. We hold on to the truth that you are with us wherever we go (Joshua 1:9).

Protect us from any attack and shield us from the enemy's plan. Fill us with your presence and reassurance, knowing that your presence is our greatest strength and comfort. Encourage our hearts and minds. Remind us of your constant support and guidance. Please help us to stand firm and have faith and confidence in your protection and presence.

In Jesus' name, we pray.

Amen

Gideon was Empowered in Weakness

Gideon: Empowered in Weakness

Judges, chapters 6 - 7

Gideon's story is a powerful example of God empowering the unlikely, initially hiding and doubtful. Gideon was called to deliver Israel from the Midianites. Despite his fears, God gave Gideon the assurance and signs he needed. With a mere 300 men, God empowered Gideon to defeat a vast army, illustrating that God's power is perfect in our weakness.

But he said to me, "My grace is sufficient for you, for my power is made perfect in weakness." Therefore I will boast all the more gladly about my weaknesses, so that Christ's power may rest on me.

- 2 Corinthians 12:9

Personal Weakness

Gideon felt inadequate and unworthy of God's task. In Judges 6:15, he expresses his sense of weakness and insignificance. Oh, my Lord, how can I save Israel? Indeed, my clan is weak in Manasseh, and I am released from my father's house.

He felt he was the least likely person to lead Israel and questioned his ability to fulfill God's calling.

Situational Weakness

Getting in was facing a complicated and seemingly impossible situation. The Midianites were oppressing the Israelites, and Gideon's clan was weak and impoverished, adding to his sense of helplessness. Despite these weaknesses, God assured Gideon that He would be with him and give him the strength to overcome the challenges. This demonstrates how God's power is made perfect in our weakness as He provides the strength and assurance needed to fulfill His purpose.

For the Spirit God gives us does not make us timid, but gives us power, love and self-discipline.
  - 2 Timothy 1:7

Encouragement and Moments of Weakness
Embrace Your Weakness

Just as Gideon felt inadequate and questioned his abilities, we all experience moments of weakness. It's important to remember that these moments are not a reflection of our worth but an opportunity for God to demonstrate His power. As 2 Corinthians 12:9 says, *"But he said to me, 'My grace is sufficient for you and my strength is made perfect in weakness.'"*

Trust in God's Promises

God promises to be with us even when we feel at our lowest. Isaiah 41:10 reassures us, *"Fear not, for I am with you; be not be dismayed, for I am your God. I will strengthen you. Yes. I will uphold you with my righteous right hand."*

God's presence and support are unwavering, no matter our Circumstances. There were times when I faced disciplinary action at work. At the time, I felt it was an unjust attack by the enemy. The action threatened and undermined my position. I felt like I couldn't move forward, and my hopes were dashed. Except for God, even in these challenging times, I experienced God's incredible strength and support. Despite my circumstances, He gave me the courage and resilience to navigate the situation. With the Holy Spirit's guidance, I could overcome the obstacles and bypass the enemy's plans. God's strength was evident as I remained steadfast and focused on his promises. This promise became a reality for me during the hardest of times.

Let's Pray!

A Prayer for Strength in Weakness

Heavenly Father,

I come before you, acknowledging my weaknesses and limitations. Just as you empowered Gideon in his moments of doubt and fear, I ask that you strengthen me in my weakness. I often feel inadequate and unworthy, questioning whether I can accomplish what you've called me to do. But I know that your grace is sufficient, and in my weakness, your power is made perfect.

Lord, when I feel small and incapable, remind me of your promises. Fill me with the confidence that you are with me, just as you were with Gideon. Help me to embrace my weakness, not as a hindrance, but as an opportunity for you to show your strength. May your Spirit empower me with courage, love, and self-discipline, guiding me through every challenge I face.

I trust in your word, Lord, that says, "Fear not, for I am with you." Let your presence be my assurance in times of uncertainty. Uphold me with your righteous hand and give me the faith to rely on your strength rather than my own. When circumstances seem overwhelming and I feel oppressed, remind me that your power will carry me through.

Thank you for using me, even in my weakest moments. Let your grace and strength shine through, making me a testimony of your faithfulness.

In Jesus' name, I pray.

Amen

David: Empowered for Victory

1 Samuel chapter 17

As a young shepherd, David faced Goliath. A warrior with nothing but a sling and faith in God, David's empowerment came from his unwavering trust in God's deliverance. His victory over Goliath showed that God empowers those who trust him regardless of their size or experience.

David was Confident

The Lord is my light and my salvation—

whom shall I fear?

The Lord is the stronghold of my life—

of whom shall I be afraid?
   - Psalm 27:1

The story of David's victory over Goliath is one of the most famous examples of God's power working through an individual faith and courage. Just as David, a young shepherd, faced the giant Goliath with faith and courage, I turned to God for strength and guidance. David declared in 1 Samuel 17:45, *"You come to me with a sword, with a spear, and with a javelin. But I come to you in the name of the Lord of hosts, the God of the armies of Israel, whom you have defied." (NKJV).* David trusted not in his own power but in God's might.

In my work situation, I relied on God's strength to bypass the enemy's plan. Despite the unfair treatment, God gave me the resilience to stand firm and the wisdom to navigate the challenges. Just as David's faith led to his victory over Goliath, my trust in God led to a great win in my professional life, and the disciplinary action that the enemy had planned for me was overturned. I emerged more assertive and more confident in God's provision. What a mighty God we serve!!!!

God knows exactly how to put a stop to the enemy's schemes. His intervention was apparent as he guided me through the situation, and I emerged more robust, bold, and confident in God's provision and protection. This experience has taught me that no matter the enemy's plans, God is always in control and knows how to bring those plans to an end. As Psalm 33:10-11 says, *"The Lord brings the counsel of the nations to nothing; He makes the plans of the peoples of no effect. The council of the Lord stands forever. The plans of His heart to all generations." (NKJV)*

Facing the Giants

Have you ever faced a "GIANT" in your life? A situation that seemed impossible to overcome? What was it, and how did you initially feel?

Finding Strength

In the face of this giant, where did you find your strength? Did you rely on your abilities or turn to God for help like David?

Experiencing God's Protection

Can you recall a time when you felt God's hands of protection over you during a challenging situation? How did you experience his presence and support?

Witness God's Intervention

How has your faith helped you overcome challenges in your life? Are there specific scriptures or prayers that have been particularly meaningful to you during these tough times?

Let Me Encourage You

Then Peter began to speak: "I now realize how true it is that God does not show favoritism but accepts from every nation the one who fears him and does what is right."
- Acts 10:34-35

This means that the same strength and guidance He provides to me, He is willing to provide to each one of you. God's help will love. Are available to all of us. I want to take a moment to encourage you, especially those facing complex challenges and feeling overwhelmed. It feels like the enemy is working against us.

Let's Pray!

A Prayer to Face Giants in Our Lives

Heavenly Father,

We come before you, seeking your strength and guidance. We trust in your power to stop the enemy's plan and lead us through every challenge. Help us remain steadfast in our faith, knowing that you are with us and show no partiality. Your help is available to us all. We thank you for your hand of protection that is always over us, just as it was with David when he faced Goliath.

In Jesus' name, we pray.

Amen

Esther: Empowered for Such a Time as This

Esther 4:12-16

Queen Esther's story highlights the empowerment that comes from courage and strategic action. Faced with the potential destruction of her people, Esther risks her life to approach the King. Her boldness and faith led to the salvation of the Jews, teaching us that God empowers us to act with courage in critical moments.

How Can We Be Like Esther?

...in whom we have boldness and access with confidence through our faith in Him.

- Ephesians 3:12 (NKJV)

Have Faith in God's Plan

Proverbs 3:5-6 encourages us, *"Trust in the Lord with all your heart and lean not on your own understanding; in all your ways submit to him, and he will make your paths straight."*

Esther trusted that God had a purpose for her life even when she couldn't see the full picture. We can follow her example by believing that God has a plan for each of us, even under challenging circumstances.

Seek God's Guidance

If any of you lacks wisdom, you should ask God, who gives generously to all without finding fault, and it will be given to you.
- James 1:5

Act with Boldness

"For if you remain silent at this time, relief and deliverance for the Jews will arise from another place, but you and your father's family will perish. And who knows but that you have come to your royal position for such a time as this?"
- Esther 4:14

Esther's boldness came from her conviction that she was in her position for a purpose. We, too, are placed in specific situations for a purpose. Let us act boldly, trusting that God has equipped us for the task He has given us.

Let's Pray!

A Prayer to Follow God No Matter What

Heavenly Father,

I come before you with a heart seeking courage and strength, just as you empowered Esther for her moment of purpose. Like Esther, I want to trust in your divine plan for my life, even when I can't see the whole picture. Help me to have unwavering faith in your guidance and not lean on my understanding but trust that you are directing my path.

Lord, grant me the wisdom to seek your will in everything I do. When I face difficult decisions or moments of uncertainty, remind me that you generously give wisdom to those who ask. Lead me to make choices that align with your purpose and reflect your love and righteousness.

Give me the boldness that Esther had, Lord. Help me act confidently, knowing that you have placed me exactly where I am for a reason. Just as Esther was called for "such a time as this," I know that you have equipped me for the challenges and opportunities before me. May I step forward in faith, courageously trusting that you will provide everything I need to fulfill your calling.

Thank you, Father, for being with me every step of the way, just as you were with Esther. Strengthen my heart, fill me with boldness, and let my actions bring glory to your name.

In Jesus' mighty name, I pray.

Amen

Peter and John: Empowered to Witness

Acts, chapters 3 - 4

In the New Testament, the Holy Spirit empowered Peter and John to perform miracles and boldly proclaim the Gospel. Despite facing threats and imprisonment, their unwavering faith and empowerment by the Holy Spirit enabled them to continue their mission, demonstrating the transformative power of God's Spirit in believers.

The Early Church: Empowered by the Holy Spirit

Acts, chapter 2

The day of Pentecost marked a pivotal moment of empowerment for the early Church. The Holy Spirit descended upon the apostles, enabling them to speak different languages and boldly share the Gospel. This empowerment ignited the spread of Christianity and demonstrated the power of the Holy Spirit to equip and encourage believers.

These biblical examples illustrate that God empowers those He calls, providing them with the strength, courage, and resources needed to fulfill His purpose. As you read these stories, be encouraged that the same God who empowered Moses, Joshua, Gideon, David, Esther, Peter, John, and the Early Church is ready to empower you today!!! Trust in His promises, step in faith and experience His transformative power.

Let's Pray!

Heavenly Father,

I come before you with a humble heart, seeking the same boldness and strength you gave Peter and John. Empower me, Lord, with the courage to witness to others just as they did. Fill me with the Holy Spirit, that I may be fearless in sharing your truth, even in the face of challenges or opposition. Like Peter and John, please give me the strength to stand firm in my faith, unwavering in my mission to proclaim the Gospel.

Lord, I ask for the power of your Spirit to work through me, just as it did through Peter and John, who performed miracles and spoke with boldness because of their faith in you. Let me be a vessel of your transformative power so that I may touch the lives of others with your love, grace, and truth.

Like the apostles, please help me be steadfast even when faced with trials. When I am challenged or misunderstood, remind me of their example—that through the power of your Holy Spirit, I can overcome every obstacle in Jesus' name. Empower me to carry out the mission you've set before me, not by my own strength but by the strength you provide.

Thank you, Father, for the empowerment you offer to all believers. Let me be a witness to your grace and truth in every area of my life.

In Jesus' name, I pray.

Amen

Reflection

Moses: Empowered to Lead

Despite Moses' feelings of inadequacy, God equipped him to lead the Israelites out of Egypt. His strength was not in his abilities but in God's presence.

Have you ever felt unqualified for something God called you to do? How might His presence give you the strength to move forward?

Joshua: Empowered with Courage

Joshua faced incredible challenges, yet God's command to "be strong and courageous" gave him the confidence to lead. God's constant presence was his assurance.

In what areas of your life do you need to embrace God's courage and trust His presence is with you?

Gideon: Empowered in Weakness

Gideon, feeling unworthy and weak, was empowered by God to defeat the Midianites. This demonstrates that God's strength is made perfect in our weakness.

How can you rely on God's strength when you feel weak or overwhelmed by your circumstances?

David: Empowered for Victory

David's victory over Goliath was rooted in his faith in God's power, not his strength. His trust in God made the impossible possible.

What "giant" are you facing, and how can you trust God for victory?

Esther: Empowered for Such a Time as This

Esther's boldness in risking her life to save her people shows that God empowers us to act with courage and faith when we are placed in crucial moments.

Is there a situation in your life where God is calling you to step out in faith and boldness?

How does Esther's story give you strength to face the uncertainties of walking out what God commissioned you to do?

Peter and John: Empowered to Witness

Peter and John, filled with the Holy Spirit, boldly proclaimed the Gospel even in the face of threats. Their courage came from the empowerment of God's Spirit.

How can you let the Holy Spirit empower you to be bold in sharing your faith, even when it's uncomfortable?

The Early Church: Empowered by the Holy Spirit

The Holy Spirit's descent at Pentecost empowered the apostles to spread the Gospel and transform lives, demonstrating that God equips those He calls.

How might you open yourself up to the Holy Spirit's empowerment in your everyday life?

Chapter 7

Perseverance and Endurance

Staying Strong in Faith Amidst Trials

We can be sure of one thing: we will face challenges and trials that will test our faith and push us to our limits. The enemy will try to steal our hope, joy, faith, and even our lives, if he can. We must stay strong and cling to God even when the storm is fiercest. We must persevere and push through with God. It is the only way. Perseverance is a crucial aspect of the Christian faith. It is the ability to endure hardship and maintain steadfastness in our belief despite our challenges. As believers, we are not promised a life free from trials and tribulations. Instead, we are sure God will be with us, empowering us to persevere and endure.

Trust in God's Plan

And we know that in all things God works for the good of those who love him, who have been called according to his purpose.
- Romans 8:28

Even when we don't understand why we're facing specific trials, we can trust that God has a purpose and a plan for our lives.

Seek God's Presence

God is our refuge and strength, an ever-present help in trouble.
- Psalm 46:1

Amid trials, draw near to God through prayer, worship, and reading His Word. Always remember that God is our refuge and strength. He is always there to help us in trouble.

Keep an Eternal Perspective

I consider that our present sufferings are not worth comparing with the glory that will be revealed in us.
- Romans 8:18

Remember that our present suffering is not worthy compared with the glory that will be revealed in us. Fixing our eyes on Jesus and the hope of eternal life helps us to endure temporary hardship.

William Wilberforce: A Life of Perseverance for Justice

There is a story I would like to share with you of a man who was known for his faith and perseverance that you may not know of. One powerful story of perseverance with God in history is that of William Wilberforce, the British politician and social reformer who led the abolition of the transatlantic slave trade.

Born in 1759, Wilberforce came to faith in Christ in his mid-20s, dramatically transforming his worldview. He saw his position as a Member of Parliament as a platform to serve God and humanity. In 1787, he began a tireless campaign to abolish the British slave trade, which was responsible for the horrific treatment and enslavement of millions of Africans.

Wilberforce faced immense opposition. The slave trade was deeply embedded in the British economy, and many powerful interests, including politicians, merchants, and even religious leaders, resisted his efforts. Year after year, his bills to abolish the slave trade were defeated in Parliament. He endured ridicule, personal attacks, and threats to his health. On several occasions, he contemplated giving up the fight, yet his faith in God and his conviction that slavery was a moral evil kept him going.

Encouraged by his friends, including John Newton (a former slave trader turned abolitionist and the author of the hymn "Amazing Grace"), Wilberforce persisted for nearly 20 years. Finally, in 1807, after years of effort and perseverance, the British Parliament passed the Abolition of the Slave Trade Act, making the transatlantic slave trade illegal.

Even after this victory, Wilberforce continued to fight for the complete emancipation of all enslaved people in the British Empire, which was eventually achieved in 1833—just three days before his death.

Let's Pray!

Prayer to Remain Steadfast

Heavenly Father,

We come before you with a humble heart, seeking your strength and guidance as we navigate through the trials and challenges of life. You are our refuge and our fortress, our ever-present help in times of trouble. We thank you for your unwavering love and faithfulness. Lord, we ask for your divine strength to remain steadfast in our faith when we must persevere. Just as you empowered Moses, Job, Joseph, David, Paul, and so many others, we ask you, please, Lord Jesus Christ, empower us with your Holy Spirit. He fills us with the courage and endurance we must face daily. When we feel overwhelmed and have weary spirits, remind us of our promises. Help us trust your plan even when we do not understand it. Our circumstances teach us to lean on you for support, knowing that you are with us every step of the way.

In Jesus' name.

Amen

Reflection

Wilberforce's life shows the power of perseverance, faith, and obedience to God's call, even in the face of overwhelming opposition. His commitment to justice, inspired by his Christian faith, brought about a profound social change that transformed the lives of millions.

In what areas of your life is God calling you to persevere, even when the road seems long and difficult? How can you trust His timing and strength to carry you through?

Chapter 8

Embracing your Journey

As I come to the end of this book, I invite you to take a moment to reflect on your journey. We've explored the depths of spiritual empowerment, learned about incredible weapons and our warfare, and examined the lives of biblical figures who face trials with unwavering faith. Now it's time to embrace this journey with confidence and hope, knowing that God is with you every step of the way and has great plans for your life. Trust in His promises, walk His empowerment, and live for His glory.

Understanding the Journey

Life as a believer is a journey filled with highs and lows, victories and challenges.

It's a path of continuous growth where our faith is tested and strengthened. This journey isn't always easy, but it's one of our most rewarding experiences. Embracing this journey means accepting both the joys and the trials. Trusting that

God uses every experience to mold us into the person he created us to be.

We must embrace our new identity in Christ. Understanding who we are in Christ is foundational to embracing our journey. We are beloved children of God, redeemed by the blood of Jesus and empowered by the Holy Spirit. Our identity in Christ assures us that we are never alone. No matter what we face, we can stand firm in the knowledge of God our Father, Jesus our Savior, and the Holy Spirit, our comforter and guide.

As I conclude this journey, I want to extend an invitation to anyone who may not Yet have a personal relationship with Jesus Christ. The journey of faith begins with a single step, opening your heart to the love and grace of Jesus. This decision is the most important one you will ever make, and it has the power to transform your life in ways you could never imagine. Salvation is a gift from God when we confess our sins and place our trust in Jesus Christ as our Lord and Savior; we are forgiven and given the gift of eternity.

Let's Pray!

A Simple Prayer of Salvation

Dear God,

I recognize that I am a sinner and that my sin separates me from you. I believe that Jesus Christ, your Son, died on the cross for my sins and rose from the dead. I confess my sin and ask for your forgiveness. I invite Jesus into my heart as my Savior and make Him Lord of my life. Help me to live for you and follow your ways. Thank you for the gift of eternal life!

In Jesus' name.

Amen!

This is the next step in your journey. If you prayed this prayer and accepted Jesus as your Lord and Savior...congratulations! You have made the most critical decision of your life. Here are some next steps to help you grow.

Read the Bible

Pray Regularly

Join a Church Community

Ask others to help you live out your faith.

Tell others about the wonderful Kingdom of God, Jesus's love, and the abundant life He has for them!

Reflection

What has been the most significant spiritual truth you've encountered throughout this book, and how does it apply to your current journey?

In what ways has your understanding of spiritual empowerment and your identity in Christ grown or changed?

How have the trials and victories in your life shaped your relationship with God?

What role does faith play in your daily struggles and suc-
cesses?

Are there specific areas of your life where God is calling you
to trust Him more deeply? What might it look like to surrender those areas to Him?

If you are already on this faith journey, how can you encourage others just beginning their walk with Christ? If you're
just starting, what steps can you take to strengthen your relationship with Jesus?

Looking ahead, how can you continue to embrace both the joys and challenges of your journey, trusting that God has a purpose for every season of your life?

In light of this chapter's invitation to salvation, what steps do you feel prompted to take next in your faith journey?

How can you live out the call to walk in God's empowerment and share it with others?

Next Steps as a Spirit-filled Christian

If someone wants to become a Christian and join a Spirit-filled church that believes in the baptism of the Holy Spirit, here are some common next steps they might take:

1. Accepting Jesus Christ as Lord and Savior

Prayer of Salvation:

The journey begins with a personal decision to accept Jesus as their Lord and Savior, confessing their sins, and asking for forgiveness. This is often done through a simple prayer of salvation.

Repentance and Faith:

Repenting from past sins and choosing to follow Jesus in faith is central to this decision.

2. Baptism in Water

Public Declaration:

Water baptism is a public demonstration of their new faith in Christ, symbolizing the death of their old life and resurrection into new life in Jesus.

Joining a Baptism Class:

Many churches offer baptism classes to help believers understand the significance of baptism and prepare for it.

3. Receiving the Baptism of the Holy Spirit

Teaching on the Baptism of the Holy Spirit:

Many Spirit-filled churches provide teachings on the Baptism of the Holy Spirit, explaining its role in the believer's life.

Praying to Receive:

Believers pray to receive the baptism of the Holy Spirit, which may be accompanied by the evidence of speaking in tongues, prophetic words, or other spiritual gifts.

Impartation:

In some churches, laying on of hands by church leaders or members is part of the prayer for the Baptism of the Holy Spirit.

4. Joining a Spirit-filled Church Community

Attend Services Regularly:

Becoming a part of the church community is vital for spiritual growth. Regular attendance allows the person to be discipled and grow in fellowship with other believers.

Spirit-led Worship:

Spirit-filled churches often emphasize worship that invites the presence of the Holy Spirit, such as extended times of praise, prophetic worship, and open altars for prayer.

Bible Study and Prayer Groups:

Joining Bible studies and prayer groups helps new believers grow in their understanding of Scripture and spiritual gifts.

5. Developing Spiritual Gifts

Learning About Spiritual Gifts:

Spirit-filled churches typically teach about spiritual gifts like prophecy, healing, tongues, interpretation of tongues, and discerning of spirits.

Discovering Your Gifts:

Many churches offer courses or mentorship programs to help new believers discover and use their spiritual gifts for ministry within the church and community.

6. Discipleship and Mentorship

Discipleship Programs:

Many Spirit-filled churches offer structured discipleship programs in which new believers are paired with mentors who guide them in their walk with Christ.

One-on-One Mentoring:

A mentor helps guide new Christians through the challenges of their faith journey by providing personal support and prayer.

7. Daily Spiritual Practices

Prayer and Devotion:

Growing in a personal relationship with God through daily prayer, reading the Bible, and worshiping at home is foundational.

Listening to the Holy Spirit:

Spirit-filled churches encourage believers to cultivate a relationship with the Holy Spirit, learning to listen and obey His voice in their daily lives, just as Jesus did when He was a man on Earth.

8. Engaging in Ministry and Service

Serving in the Church:

Spirit-filled churches often encourage believers to get involved in ministry, using their gifts to serve in areas like worship, prayer teams, teaching, or outreach.

Outreach and Evangelism:

Many Spirit-filled churches emphasize sharing the gospel and reaching out to others through evangelism and mission work.

These steps help new believers grow spiritually, become part of the church body, and walk in the power of the Holy Spirit.

Printed in the USA
CPSIA information can be obtained
at www.ICGtesting.com
LVHW011533121124
796419LV00037B/717

* 9 7 8 1 9 6 5 0 5 0 0 2 6 *